FACTS AND IMPACT OF 27 NAKSHATRAS

DR. JAGADEESH PILLAI

!! Humble dedication to Astrology Lovers around the world !!

Contents

Contents

Prayer

Oṃ bhūr bhuvaḥ suvaḥ

tat savitur vareṇyaṃ

bhargo devasya dhīmahi

dhiyo yo naḥ prachodayāt

About The Author

Dr. Jagadeesh Pillai four times Guinness World Record holder, a voracious reader, writer, and true research scholar was born in Varanasi, the abode of Lord Shiva. He is Ph.D. in Vedic Science. He is a multi-faceted polymath with innate qualities, creative ideas and many remarkable achievements. Although his roots extend back to "Gods own Country"(Kerala), the residents of Varanasi feel proud of him and adore him as a child of Varanasi who caters to every individual in need without any expectations. A deep study into his profile reflects that he has added so many feathers to his cap which makes him quite unique. He is a four times Guinness Book of World Records Holder in the following subjects :

1. "Script to Screen" which he achieved by producing and directing a state of art animation film within the shortest time possible by breaking the earlier set record by Canadians. There are many national and international Awards and Recognitions to his credit.

2. Longest Line of Post Cards which he has done on the occasion of 163 years of Indian Postal Day by 16300 post cards. The event was also connected with a questionnaire about Indian Flag.

3. Largest Poster Awareness Campaign – This was achieved by designing an awareness campaign on the subject "Beti Bachao – Beti Padhao".

4. Largest Envelop – Towards tribute to Prime Minister's

initiative 'Make in India' – he has created about 4000 sq meter envelop using waste papers.

5. Attempted by lighting 70000 candles on a 210 kg cake to celebrate the 70th Indian Independence day recorded in World Records India.

6. Attempted a documentary on Dhamek Stupa of Sarnath dubbing in 17 languages, result is waiting from Guinness World Records.

He is versatile in Gita teaching. The young generation is fond of his Gita teaching and he has changed the life of many young through his continued motivational boost up and teachings.

He has composed and sung Gayatri Mantra in 1008 different tunes.

He has composed and sung Hanuman Chalisa in 108 different tunes.

He has composed and sung hundreds of Sanskrit Bhajans, Patriotic songs, etc.

He has written and directed so many short films and documentaries for awareness campaigns.

He has done voluntary services to UP Police and Kerala Police to spread awareness campaigns on the various issue through videos and photography.

He is on the path of authoring thousands of books on Indian culture, Indian Temples, and the life of extraordinary people.

It is hard to believe that he has produced and directed more than 100 Documentaries on a particular city (Varanasi) which is done by a single person.

He has helped and guided more than 25 boys and girls to achieve world records through various creative and innovative methods.

A multifaceted person who can apply the best of his intellect using the God-given blessings which have been showered upon every human being granting them an immense capacity to learn, experience, and experiment with many things and do wonders in this world of discrimination and disparities.

He is a teacher and a student at the same time who always learns every day and teaches every day. As a master, his weakness was that he never sticks to a particular subject. Perhaps this weakness gives him the strength to master any area which he came across.

Each of his days dawned with learning a new topic and he spend most of his time experimenting and researching it.

He is also a selfless social activist and a motivational speaker.

His life was full of struggle, ups and downs, and failures.

But he never gave up and faced all his trials and tribulations full of confidence. Today he is a successful young man with a lot of enthusiasm and rich life experience.

He has sung full Ram Charita Manas 51 hours audio by his own composition. He has also sung the whole Bhagavad-Gita in his own composition with a rhythmic background.

He has also sung "Lokah Samastha Sukhino Bhavantu" in 50 different languages.

Currently working on a detailed and scientific study on Veda, Upanishad, Puranas, Bhagavad Gita, etc.

He has composed and sung Hanuman Chalisa in 108 different compositions and Gayatri Mantra in 1008 different compositions.

Awards

Four Times Guinness World Records

Winner of Mahatma Gandhi Vishwa Shanti Puraskar

Mahatma Gandhi Global Peace Ambassador

Kashi Ratna Award

Dr. APJ Abdul Kalam Motivational Person of the Year 2017

Mother Teresa Award

Indira Gandhi Priyadarshini Award

ABOUT THE AUTHOR

Bharat Vikas Ratna Award

Udyog Ratna Award

• xiii •

Vigyan Prasar Award

Poorvanchal Ratn Samman

Preface

Astrology is immensely popular in the Indian continent and is considered one of the six Vedangas. The 27 Nakshatras are essential for astrological readings, and this document is intended to provide an easy reference for anyone interested in this fascinating subject. Herein, I have compiled my notes, readings, and understanding of the 27 Nakshatras.

Each nakshatra has its own unique characteristics and role in human life, depending on one's birth details. By understanding the role and nature of each nakshatra, it is possible to fine-tune our lives according to astrological readings based on nakshatras. With this knowledge, we can gain a greater insight into our own lives and the lives of those around us.

If we refer to the birth details according to astrological calculations, every human is associated with a Janma Nakshatra, and it holds great importance in our lives. This book provides a simple and comprehensive understanding of the 27 nakshatras, offering a convenient reference guide.

- Dr. Jagadeesh Pillai, PhD in Vedic Science, Four Times Guinness World Record Holder

CHAPTER ONE

FACTS AND IMPACT OF NAKSHATRAS

The 27 Nakshatras are an integral part of Hindu astrology, and they are believed to have a profound influence on the lives of individuals. Each Nakshatra is associated with a particular deity, and it is believed that the deity's energy is present in the Nakshatra. The Nakshatras are divided into four categories: the Manushya Nakshatras, the Deva Nakshatras, the Rakshasa Nakshatras, and the Gandharva Nakshatras. Each of these categories has its own unique characteristics and effects on the lives of individuals.

The Manushya Nakshatras are associated with the human realm and are believed to bring about positive changes in the lives of individuals. These Nakshatras are associated with the qualities of courage, strength, and determination. The Deva Nakshatras are associated with the divine realm and are believed to bring about spiritual growth and enlightenment. The Rakshasa Nakshatras are associated with the demonic realm and are believed to bring about negative changes in the lives of individuals. Finally, the Gandharva Nakshatras are associated with the celestial realm and are believed to bring about harmony and balance in the lives of individuals.

The 27 Nakshatras are believed to have a powerful influence on the lives of individuals. Each Nakshatra is associated with a particular deity, and it is believed that the deity's energy is present in the Nakshatra. It is believed that the Nakshatras can bring about positive changes in the lives of individuals, such as courage, strength, and spiritual growth. They can also bring about negative changes, such as fear, anger, and disharmony. It is important to understand the impact of the Nakshatras on one's life in order to make the most of their potential.

CHAPTER TWO

NAKSHATRAS IN ASTROLOGY

Nakshatras, or asterisms, or astrological lunar mansions, are one of the most integral aspects of Indian astrology. There are 27 nakshatras, starting from Ashwini and ending with Revati, each representing energies present in the universe to direct human progress and behavior.

Nakshatras are believed to have significant prophetic meaning, governing destinies of humans since ancient times. The ancient Hindu scripture, Rig Veda, contains several references to the association between constellations and character traits. Thus, these asterisms were likely used for charting purposes even in such ancient times.

Nakshatras are divided into four parts, with each part being equal to three degrees and twenty minutes of arc. This arc accounts for the separation of the nine planets from each other. A person's birth chart is determined by the combination of Nakshatra, along with the Rashi and Paada.

The Nakshatra is an important factor in determining a person's character, talents and destiny. Each nakshatra has unique characteristics, and these characteristics manifest in the individual born under that nakshatra. The nakshatra gives an insight into one's mental, physical and spiritual traits and tendencies. The strength of these tendencies determine the course of one's life.

Nakshatras are an integral part of Vedic astrology, and can enhance the accuracy in readings and predictions. The Nakshatras are attributed to forces of nature, and focus on the traits and instincts of the individual. The nakshatra indicates the role the person is meant to play in the world, and how that role can be served most effectively.

The Nakshatras also indicate the timing of important life events such as marriage, childbirth, health matters, financial matters, and so on. The exact dates and times of these events can be determined more accurately by consulting the Nakshatras. The Nakshatras thus offer insight into when these important events may take place and help one plan for these events accordingly.

Overall, Nakshatras are integral to Indian astrology and offer insight into the deeper aspects of a person's personality and destiny. With their depth of information, they can help in charting a successful future that is in alignment with one's true purpose in life.

CHAPTER THREE

NAKSHATRAS AND ZODIAC SIGNS

In astrology, there are two primary celestial objects which are used to measure events which occur on Earth, Nakshatras and Zodiac signs. Each system is seen to be working in harmony with the other, as one marks points in the sky for certain zodiac houses, while the other marks within these points various asterisms known as Nakshatras. Therefore, one cannot be discussed without mentioning the other.

Nakshatras, unlike Zodiac signs, are stars or asterisms that form a specific pattern in the night sky, and which humans all over the world have observed since ancient times. Concomitantly, the Nakshatra system is based upon the stars that were seen by ancient cultures and is the oldest form of astrological classification. However, in the astrology of India, the Nakshatras derive strong significance as they are named after and associated with various gods and goddesses of the Hindu pantheon. In Vedic astrology, each Nakshatra is associated with distinct attributes which are believed to be revealed in an individual's behaviour, traits, and conditions one faces in life

The Zodiac signs on the other hand, are described in terms of the month-long portions of the sky, which are thought to have an influence on the people born during a particular month. In the Western zodiac system, there are 12 unique segments which are named after animals and which form the basis for the division of the calendar year. A person is said to be born and fall under the sign they are birthed into that particular month. It is believed that general characteristics of those Zodiac signs remain to be true throughout the calendar year.

Thus, the essential differences between these two ancient astrological systems are that Nakshatras are related to individual stars and goddesses, whereas the zodiac signs are connected to animals and 12 different months in a year. Furthermore, a more complex difference between them is that the zodiac system is used to measure division within a period of time (a month) throughout the year, whereas Nakshatras measure a point in time which is determined when an individual is born.

In conclusion, there are distinct differences between the two systems of astrology. Nakshatras are related to individual stars and Hindu deities while the Zodiac signs are associated with animals and months of the year. Moreover, Nakshatra astrology is primarily used to measure a moment in time while, with the help of the Zodiac system, a division of time throughout a year is measured, based on one's birth month.

CHAPTER FOUR

MYTH BEHIND THE NAKSHATRAS IN ASTROLOGY

The mythological tale behind the Nakshatras in Astrology dates back thousands of years. It can be traced back to ancient Vedic texts, in which the 27 stars of the Zodiac were given a special significance. Astrological Nakshatras are the traditional constellations, or stars, of the Hindu and Vedic tradition, which are used to measure the movement of planets and calculate the destiny of mankind.

The story behind these Nakshatras gives a deeper insight into the great importance given to them. According to an ancient Vedic myth, the arrangement of the Nakshatras was done by the Hindu god Vishnu, who was ordered by the creator god, Brahma, to create the constellations of the Zodiac to measure time and help guide spiritual practice.

At the same time, a demon called Matar was sent forth by the same god. Matar was to distribute, with Vishnu's help, all the knowledge and wisdom to mankind. In order to do this, Matar created the Nakshatras to govern the four directions of the sky, one for each season.

These Nakshatras were also believed to be symbols for the Vedic deities, who in turn represented virtues such as strength, knowledge, or prosperity, and were thus given names such as Arundhati, Abhijit, and Bharathi, each signifying a particular motive.

The alignment of the Nakshatras was, therefore, said to affect the lives of those living in accordance with them. People have believed that to have good luck and fortune, it is essential to have a strong alignment of the constellations, which will bring peace, prosperity and success. It is said that the Nakshatras also guide the path of spiritual success, helping people realize their potential in life.

Additionally, in Indian Astrology, Nakshatras are used to decode the current and intended events of an individual's life. Thus, Nakshatras play an important role in astrology and derive their power from the ancient mythological tale outlined in Vedic texts.

In conclusion, the Nakshatras of Astrology are interlinked with an ancient mythological tale, giving them a unique and powerful meaning. This meaning is still relevant today as it links with astrological practices used to interpret life's events.

CHAPTER FIVE

ASHWINI NAKSHTRA

(1 - Ashwathi)

Ashwini Nakshatra is one of the 27 Nakshatras in Hindu mythology and astrology. Nakshatras are used to calculate horoscope and other important aspects related to astrology. The Ashwini nakshatra in particular has some wholesome significance in astrology. Specifically it is very important for determining the planetary positions in a given horoscope.

This Nakshatra is symbolized by a horse individually representing strength and vigour and mythology states that when the divine horse emerged from the sea containing the fourteen gems, these gems formed the basis of the Ashwini Nakshatra. The Ashwini Nakshatra is located in the constellation Aries and it reigns from 0°-13°20 in Aries. Four main stars make up this nakshatra and they are Aries, Cursa, Botein and Hamal.

Astrology believes Ashwini Nakshatra is a sign of luck and prosperousness. People under its influence are believed to possess unusual intelligence, ambition, determination and positivity. They are also believed to enjoy the support of family, friends and society and are consequently successful in life. They are rebellious and independent in nature and their potentials should not be underestimated.

Another major role the Ashwini Nakshatra plays in astrology is in determining the muhurthas, or auspicious times for ceremonies such as marriages. It is believed that when the Moon is in the Ashwini Nakshatra, the chances of success for all activities that are planned for that time are higher. It also indicates career progress, travel and all other major life decisions.

In terms of struggles and losses, it is said that people under the influence of the Ashwini Nakshatra can suffer from diminished enthusiasm and energy, leading to some uncomfortable delays and obstacles in life. But this can be fixed by performing appropriate remedial measures according to astrology and consulting the experts about it.

In conclusion, Ashwini Nakshatra holds much significance in the world of astrology and is a strong omen of success and prosperity. Its presence ensures good luck, professionalism, and ambition in one's life. These can be further enhanced by consulting astrological experts to get the best of astrological advice.

CHAPTER SIX

BHARANI NAKSHTRA

(2 - Bharani)

Bharani Nakshatra is an important star constellation in Indian astrology. It is one of the 27 lunar mansions and is symbolized by the Yoni - an organ of a female deity. The Moon is considered to be the ruling planet of this star, and it has a predominantly auspicious influence over a person's life. The main characteristic of this star is great determination, setting a good example for us to trust in our hard work and ambition.

Bharani Nakshatra supports human ambition and is believed to favor the completion of difficult and challenging tasks. Those who are born under this influence are determined, courageous, and hard-working by nature. People with this star usually possess a strong will to carry out their vision and also have a good financial aptitude. Their mental strength and focus is admirable, which helps them overcome obstacles in life and achieve success in their endeavors.

Bharani Nakshatra has a direct impact on the destiny of an individual. It is believed that this star can either give beneficial results or destructive results, depending on other planetary influences. Those benefitting from this star's energy will experience happiness, success, and growth in their life. Whereas, those who are negatively influenced will face difficulties and hardships throughout.

In terms of astrology, this star is used to analyze a person's destiny, troubles, and lifestyle. The positive and auspicious connection between this star and other planets is believed to bring a certain degree of strength and determination to overcome any sort of unfavourable situation. A careful analysis of the positions of this star in the birth-chart can even provide guidance in planning a course of action that can bring success in ventures and initiatives.

Furthermore, this star is known for providing a good measure of life-force and has a strong influence on the power of attraction. It also has an influence on partnership and partnerships of all kinds, whether between husband and wife, business partners, or even siblings.

In conclusion, Bharani Nakshatra is an important star in Indian astrology which has a great influence on one's destiny, strength, and life-integrity. It helps an individual focus their energies in the right direction and provides them the much-needed determination they require to achieve their goals. While the strength of its effects depend on other planetary influences, this star is mostly considered benefitting and assists in leading a happy and successful life.

KRITTIKA NAKSHATRA

(3 - Karthika)

The Krittika Nakshatra is one of the oldest, most widely known, and influential aspects of Vedic Astrology. Valued for its precision and accuracy, it is used to analyze the current planetary positions, developing trends, and potential outcomes of a person's life. The impact of Krittika Nakshatra on an individual's life is profound, as the Krittika Nakshatra not only has the power to reveal the truth about a person's destiny but also the potential to shape and dictate future events.

Krittika Nakshatra is defined by a field of stars located between 23°20 and 26°40 in the Ashwini constellation. This span makes up the territory occupied by the Krittika Nakshatra. As part of this constellation, Krittika is associated with several deities and symbolic images, including Agni, Deivi, Goddess Anjana, and an image of a motherly figure carrying a staff and a water pot. Krittika represents the lighting of a bonfire and symbolizes the power of Lord Agni, which is associated with the sacrificial fire.

In the context of the Vedic jyotish, or astrology, Krittika Nakshatra's position in the zodiac is believed to influence the overall destiny of an individual. It is said that the person born in this region will have to experience the impact of the presence of the Krittika Nakshatra in their lives in the form of destiny and fate. To correctly assess the effects of its influence, it is important to consider all the aspects of the planet, including its placement in the natal chart, its lordship, its inherent energy, and the astrological placements of the other planets.

The primary impact of the Krittika Nakshatra is that it reveals the truth about an individual's life. It helps to identify a person's destiny, revealing whether it is likely to be positive or negative. The Nakshatra can also capture the essence of a person's nature and character, including their strength and weaknesses. It can predict the luck associated with various aspects of a person's life, such as health, career, education, and social life.

In terms of its role in the Vedic jyotish, the Krittika Nakshatra is believed to oversee the beginnings of all karmic cycles. It is said to be the starting point for the wheel of karma and is associated with the destruction of negativity and the growth of positive intentions and experiences. By identifying and rectifying any imbalance between the psychosomatic aspect of a person's life and the higher potential, it can act as an engine of change, leading to immediate betterment in the quality of life.

CHAPTER EIGHT

ROHINI NAKSHATRA

(4 - Rohini)

The Rohini Nakshatra is one of the 27 constellations (star clusters) of the Hindu Zodiac, and is of great importance in astrology. This constellation, also known as Aldebaran, is part of the Taurus constellation in the Northern Hemisphere and is said to be ruled by the Moon. The symbol associated with the Rohini Nakshatra is a chariot and the deity associated with it is Brahma, the Creator of Universe in Hinduism.

The main facts regarding this constellation are that it is the fourth Nakshatra of the Zodiac and is located on the border of Taurus in the Northern Hemisphere. The Rohini Nakshatra is divided into four quarters, called the Pada, and is associated with the stars Alcyon (α), Theta (θ), Zeta (ζ), and Eta (η). These four stars are symbolic of the four aspects of life - the physical, the mental, the emotional, and the spiritual. People born under the Rohini Nakshatra are said to be independent, creative, and well-organized.

The impact of Rohini Nakshatra on people's lives is

significant. In the traditional Hindu astrology, the Rohini Nakshatra is considered the most auspicious one out of the entire 27 constellations. The ruling deity - Brahma - is said to bless anyone who has been born under this star with intelligence, creativity and energy. The constellations are related to human characteristics and amongst all the Nakshatras, Rohini is said to have the most potent influence. It also provides good luck and safety to people who come under its influence.

The role of Rohini Nakshatra in astrology is multifaceted. It influences the personality and life of the individuals who have been born under its influence. For example, it governs the ability of an individual to be independent, inspired and creative. People who come under its influence are said to be go-getters, willing to explore new avenues and known to be very organized. It also is said to bring prosperity, ideal parenting abilities and good fortune to people coming under its influence.

The Rohini Nakshatra can also be used in Horoscope readings. When it is concerned in a certain chart, its impact on a person's life can be seen in terms of the personality traits and in the kind of partnerships they form in life. Its placement stipulates the impacts it can have - if placed in the first house, it will signify an individual who is headstrong, independent and knowledge-seeking.

The Rohini Nakshatra is of great significance in Hindu astrology and can be seen to have a major influence on the lives of people born under it. Its association with the Taurus constellation and the deity Brahma symbolizes strength, energy and creativity for any person who falls under its influence.

CHAPTER NINE

MRIGHASIRA NAKSHATRA

(5 - Makayiram)

Since ancient times, mankind has been looking up at the night sky, wondering about the stars and planets above. Each of these constellations holds a unique significance and many cultures have used astrology to interpret their meanings. One of the prominent star signs is Mrighasira Nakshatra. It is known as one of the most mystical and powerful constellations in astrology.

Mrighasira Nakshatra is one of the 27 stars which make up the Nakshatras, a set of divisions of the zodiac in Hindu astrology. Its name comes from the Sanskrit word "mriga," which means deer and "asira," which means root. This highlights its natural and nurturing aspects. It is associated with its ruler, Mars, the god of war and action. Its symbol is a flowering plant, further emphasizing its nurturing quality.

The main purpose of the Mrighasira Nakshatra is to provide people with focus, motivation and courage. People with this star sign are known for their ambitious and entrepreneurial spirit. They are great leaders and often have the endurance and ambition to succeed in everything they put their minds to, no matter how difficult. Mrighasiras are considered very responsible and often go out of their way to help those around them. They are also very open to suggestions and tend to take initiative.

People born under this star sign tend to be driven and take their own paths in life. They never settle and are highly independent. They are also known to be deep, mysterious and intuitive, with an understanding of the world beyond the five senses. Consequently, they come up with unique solutions to complex problems that no one else can come up with. Blue sapphires are believed to be the gemstone associated with this star sign.

In terms of health, Mrighasiras often have a strong physical constitution and are active. However, they need to be careful to avoid overworking themselves, as they tend to push their bodies too hard. This star sign is associated with fertility and so it is believed that Mrighasiras may find it easier to conceive children.

Ultimately, Mrighasira Nakshatra has a profound impact on individuals who fall under this star sign. People belonging to this star sign will enjoy the benefits of having a strong physical constitution, ambitious nature, intuitive mindset and fertility. They are likely to keep going towards their goals and tend to be successful in whatever they do.

ARDRA NAKSHATRA

(6 - Thiruvathira)

Ardra Nakshatra is one of the 27 Nakshatras present in Vedic astrology, which have been used for centuries to understand and gain insight into the lives and futures of people. Nakshatras refer to the divisions of the ecliptic, or the apparent path of the Sun, along which the Moon moves. According to Vedic Astrology, Ardra Nakshatra is symbolic of tears, the mother of all emotions and it is known to be associated with grief, sorrow, and deep feelings of loss.

The Ardra Nakshatra is located in the constellation of Gemini in the star group called Mrigsira, stretching from 6 degrees 40 minutes to 20 degrees in the Gemini star sign. It is ruled by the celestial deity Rahu, also known as North Lunar Node, who is known to be associated with obstacles, challenges, and delays. This constellation has the shape of a human head and is believed to be associated with the turbulent deep sea.

The Ardra Nakshatra is believed to cause many negative effects when it is badly placed in one's chart. It could lead to financial losses, obstacles in the path of success, and separation from loved ones. It may also lead to a person feeling emotionally overwhelmed due to a lack of self-control, or too much focus on the material world. Furthermore, it can cause depression and other psychological imbalances.

However, it also has a positive role to play in one's life and can provide strength to a person with its powerful energy. This can help a person to stay determined and focused, allowing him/her to overcome any challenge and achieve success. Also, under the influence of the Ardra Nakshatra, a person can become more mentally and emotionally balanced and can use his/her spiritual energy to excel in life.

Finally, the Ardra Nakshatra is said to have an intense energy that can be used for spiritual and inner progress. Those whose horoscope has a strong placement of the Ardra Nakshatra are often seen to perform well in the spiritual field, either by withdrawing from the material world completely or by being able to understand and practice the deeper meaning in life.

In conclusion, Ardra Nakshatra is an important part of Vedic Astrology and reflects the inner emotions that can be experienced in life. The energy of this Nakshatra can either prove to be a blessing for a person or a curse, depending on how it is placed in one's chart. It can bring both grief and sorrow but also strength and profound insights. It is up to each individual to make the best use of it in order to find peace and success.

CHAPTER ELEVEN

PUNARVASU NAKSHATRA

(7 - Punartham)

Punarvasu nakshatra, also known as the Renewed Star, is one of the 27 nakshatras, which are lunar constellations that are of great importance in Vedic astrology. To ancient cultures, Punarvasu was the celestial embodiment of dawn and dusk, offering the balance of creation and destruction, as well as renewal and replenishment. It holds a significant place in the cosmic calendar, offering insight into the changes taking place in the astrological influences.

Facts: Punarvasu is the seventh nakshatra in the zodiac and is associated with the star Aldebaran. It is considered to be an auspicious nakshatra and is said to be governed by the planet Jupiter and by one of the nine forms of Aditi, the Hindu goddess of abundance. This symbolic representation of renewal and replenishment is certainly apt, as its associated star constellation is said to represent a "renewed" column of stars in comparison to the other stars in its vicinity.

Impact: As previously mentioned, Punarvasu nakshatra is associated with renewal and replenishment, and this connection is reflected in its various significances. One of these is its influence on fertility, indicating the ability to nurture and support new life and also to provide a supportive and nourishing environment for growth. As a result, Punarvasu nakshatra is said to be highly beneficial for those seeking to conceive. It can also bring luck in business, as it is associated with gains, wealth and prosperity.

Role of Punarvasu nakshatra in Astrology: Punarvasu nakshatra is said to bring continuity and dependability, as well as power, authority and ability to excel. This nakshatra is also associated with good fortune and favourable outcomes, as well as heightened intellectual ability. It is also said that individuals born under this nakshatra are often very creative and have strong analytical skills. Additionally, this nakshatra is considered to be very fortunate for learning and acquiring knowledge, particularly spiritual knowledge. It can bring the capacity to think deeply and confidently and its balanced nature promotes peace and harmony.

In conclusion, Punarvasu nakshatra has a significant role to play in the realm of Vedic astrology, particularly due its influence on fertility and its connection to abundance, renewal and replenishment. This nakshatra is associated with capable individuals, who are often very creative and analytical and are known to seek knowledge and spiritual truth. All of these points to the wonderful yet subtle influence that Punarvasu nakshatra has on the astrological sphere.

PUSHYA NAKSHATRA

(8 - Pooyam)

The Pushya Nakshatra is one of the 27 Nakshatras in Hindu astrology which is known to represent abundance, nourishment, and prosperity. This star is associated with the planet Saturn and is believed to be of immense significance when compared to other Nakshatras. It is believed that Pushya Nakshatra has great effects on every individual's life and if puja and meditation is performed during this time, it can bring in immense success.

In an astrological birth chart, the Pushya Nakshatra falls in the zodiac sign of Cancer, making it an extremely significant Nakshatra to consider. Generally, the Pushya Nakshatra is known to be a favorable time period in any individual's life and the effects of this time period could be seen from the beginning of a person's life up until the very end. This Nakshatra is believed to provide blessings from ancestors and gods as well as having positive effects on the person's career, business, health, home, and wealth.

In ancient Indian scriptures, Pushya is often related to Lord

Shiva, who is known to be the god of justice and harmony. It is believed that when an individual spends time performing puja and meditation during Pushya Nakshatra, they would receive immense blessings from Lord Shiva. This time is also associated with nourishment, abundance, and care. The powerful energy from this time is believed to bring luck, prosperity, and success in every aspect of life.

In terms of its impact, the Pushya Nakshatra is believed to bring innumerable benefits to individuals who spend time worshipping in its energies. From career success to freedom from health problems, Pushya Nakshatra has the power to bless its devotees with incredible power. It is said to bring in creative energies to the individuals during its time and helps them make good decisions. Some of the benefits of this Nakshatra also include abundance of wealth and success in all domains of life, including education and career, as well as wealth and finances.

In addition to its impact, the Pushya Nakshatra is also known to have a significant role in the field of astrology. As mentioned before, this time period is associated with Saturn, the planet of justice and discipline, which means that the effects of Pushya Nakshatra can also be seen in terms of individual and collective justice. Additionally, this time period is also known to provide remedies to malefic forces and help individuals overcome distress and misfortune.

Overall, the Pushya Nakshatra has made a great impact in the world of astrology. Its association with Lord Shiva, its powerful energy, and its various benefits, the Pushya Nakshatra presents itself as an extremely significant and favorable time period that can help individuals achieve amazing success in their lives.

CHAPTER THIRTEEN

ASHLESHA NAKSHTRA

(9 - Ayilyam)

The Ashlesha Nakshatra, which is thought to have originated from an ancient concept in India, is an important part of astrology. This is a section of the zodiac that is believed to influence the fortunes and fates of those who are born when the Sun is in the constellation of Ashlesha

The Ashlesha Nakshatra is a group of stars that could be located in the constellation of Hydra, which is a large star cluster in the night sky. The Nakshatra is believed to be a facet of one's luck and future and is part of the karmic patterns.

When one is born in the Nakshatra of Ashlesha, their life is thought to have its own particular type of energy. It is said to bring intensity and considered to be an influence that is both positive and negative. It is thought to be strong, persistent and stubborn in nature, qualities that can be experienced in some of the people born in this Nakshatra. They often possess great knowledge and intelligence, as well as strength and intuitive power.

The Nakshatras are believed to have an impact on the various aspects of life such as relationships, health, wealth and career. The arrival of this Nakshatra into the life of a person can set off a dramatic period of events and can cause a strong imprint on their destiny and well-being.

The Nakshatra of Ashlesha is believed to represent both good and bad. For instance, it can also bring extreme levels of luck and good fortune, especially professionally. It is believed to give its natives the ability to understand and make sound decisions, as well as the capacity to think strategically

But, when this Nakshatra does bring out its negative traits, then it can cause a range of issues such as extreme levels of caution and pessimism, and bring about a deep sense of insecurity and a fear of failure

In the end, the ultimate effect of the Ashlesha Nakshatra on a person's life depends on their own each individual's karma and how they act in response to its arrival. Although it can bring both good and bad fortune, it is important to remember that it is ultimately up to the individual to take control of their destiny and make the most of their situation.

MAGHA NAKSHATRA

(10 - Makam)

Magha Nakshatra, also known as Magham or Magh, is a star constellation located in the early southern part of the constellation of Leo in Hindu astrology. It is the eleventh of the 27 traditional Nakshatras in Vedic astrology, corresponding to γ, δ, and ε Leonis, and spanning from 6° 40' - 20° of the zodiac in the constellation of Leo. It is governed by the deity Pitri, which represents ancestors and the spiritual knowledge of transmigration. Magha is known as the "star of honor", the "star of Majesty", or "the throne of the preserver" and is said to be a masculine, passionate, fixed, and deep constellation in the zodiac.

What is Magha Nakshatra? Magha is a Sanskrit word meaning 'great'. It is an energy-rich constellation that is associated with influence, wealth, power, and excellence. Furthermore, Magha is linked to an inner strength to get things done, courage, honor, integrity, and success. It is believed to confer the qualities of leadership, ambition, and determination in a person's life.

When a person is born under the nakshatra Magha, the powerful energies of Magha enter their life. This can bring good fortune, spiritual knowledge, contentment, leadership, material support, and prosperity. Magha is also associated with the Sun as a result of which power, authority, and traditional values are also important components of the Magha-born personality. Magha is concerned with karmic influences that set a person on their life journey and help them to become successful and reach their highest potential. In astrology, Magha helps a person to find one's true purpose and is considered a high-energy nakshatra associated with longevity and success.

Magha Nakshatra also has a significant impact on an individual's personality. People born under the Magha Nakshatra are natural leaders who are highly ambitious and determined to achieve their goals. They are often successful, powerful, and have a great deal of influence. Additionally, they have the courage and strength necessary to take charge and get things done. Due to their strong convictions, they remain confident and self-assured in the face of any kind of adversity. Furthermore, Magha natives possess excellent communication skills and a strong sense of justice, which can help them further their goals and objectives.

The influence of Magha Nakshatra plays an important role in both Vedic astrology and Jyotish astrology. According to both schools of thought, the Magha Nakshatra is related to the concept of "karma" or "deeds", which describes the essential outcomes of an individual's actions and experiences in this life.

CHAPTER FIFTEEN

PURVA PHALGUNI NAKSHATRA

(11 - Pooram)

Purva Phalguni (or Poorva Falguni) is one of the twenty-seven Nakshatras in astrology, and is known for its strong impact and influence on the lives of those born under it. The Nakshatra is associated with the constellation of Leo, and is often referred to as the "royal one".

Purva Phalguni is the eleventh Nakshatra in the Vedic zodiac system and is ruled by the planetary force of Venus. It spans 13°20' Leo to 26°40' Leo and is represented by a bed or couch and the symbol of a man. It is characterized by its strong energy of creativity, intuition, and the desire for love, beauty, and relationships.

The impact of Purva Phalguni is felt strongly in the areas of romantic relationships, home life, and creative pursuits. Those born under this Nakshatra have a strong desire for friendship, companionship, and devotion. They seek a partner who will accept and understand their need for independence and variety. They are highly creative and expressive, but can also be easily swayed by their emotions.

The role of Purva Phalguni in astrology is to provide a sense of purpose, passion, and joy in life. Those born under this Nakshatra are generally optimistic, ambitious, and open-minded. They make great leaders, entrepreneurs, and adventurers. They are often seen as naturally blessed with immense talent and intelligence.

They enjoy art and beauty deeply, although their creative nature can often be misconstrued as laziness. It is important for those under this Nakshatra to understand the impact their creative nature has on others, and to use it as a positive force rather than a source of distraction.

In conclusion, Purva Phalguni is a powerful and influential force in astrology. It has an incredible impact on the lives of those born under it, providing them with an abundance of creativity, intuition, and passion. They have a special aptitude for success, and are well equipped to lead and explore new ventures. Through understanding the facts, impact, and role of Purva Phalguni, those born under its influence can develop a greater awareness of how the Nakshatra affects their lives, and use it to their advantage.

CHAPTER SIXTEEN

UTTARA PHALGUNI NAKSHATRA

(12 - Uthram)

Fragmented from an ancient Sanskrit text, Uttara Phalguni nakshatra is one of the most widely recognized of the Sanskrit nakshatras. The star, which appears in Orion's shoulder, is thought to have been the birthplace of the gods according to Vedic mythology. Moreover, this nakshatra also has a huge impact on astrology, and its role in divination remains deeply important in many cultures.

Uttara Phalguni Nakshatra is the twelfth nakshatra in the zodiacal circle and calculation of placement in the natal chart is done with reference to the ecliptic longitude. It is the red star located at the west of Rohini, the fourth nakshatra. It is known to bring luck and good fortune to the natives who are born under it. Physically, the star is said to be a representation of fire – a fierce but powerful element that governs this nakshatra.

In astrology, Uttara Phalguni is associated with a number of qualities such as fame, power, authority, dignity, spiritual healing, and successful home life. This star is believed to represent expansive emotions of people under it, thus creating a volatile and emotional nature in them. It is also known to represent the divine force of creation, appreciation and recognition. Symbolically, the star is represented by a bed, which implies that the natives ruled by this nakshatra have a strong desire for comfort and leisure.

The role of Uttara Phalguni in one's astrological chart is quite unique and important. It can be used to evaluate the type of emotion that is likely to be dominant for the native depending on their zodiac position in relation to the start. The star is also said to have a strong influence on the energies of the native depending on where it is placed in their chart. Its energy can help to develop qualities such as intelligence, ambition and inner strength.

Overall, Uttara Phalguni is an important nakshatra that has been revered in astrology since the ancient times. Its influence on the destiny and characteristics of the people under its rule cannot be undermined. It has the power to bring invigorating energies of creativity and success and has done so for centuries. As such, its role in astrology remains important and significant.

CHAPTER SEVENTEEN

HASTA NAKSHATRA

(13 - Attham)

Hasta Nakshatra is a powerful astrological phenomena that has been recorded in ancient texts from civilizations around the world. It is believed to have a profound impact on human life, impacting many aspects like health, marriage, success, and even childbirth. When its position in one's birth chart is favorable, it is believed to bring about luck and prosperity in one's life.

The word 'Hasta' is derived from an ancient Sanskrit term which means 'hand'. It is the 13th Nakshatra of the 27 in Hindu astrology which consists of four star positions, surrounding the Lagna. The first two quarters of this star are categorized under the Kritika Nakshatra while the third and fourth quarters bear the Virgo sign.

The symbolism of this star is that of Shiva Vishnu holding their hands up in a gesture of protection and well-being. Symbolically, people find strength and comfort under its redoubtable protection.

It is believed that those born under the Hasta Nakshatra have the unique ability to convert their lack of sign-specific power into their strength and skill. Such individuals are strong, disciplined and have powerful psychic and intuitive capabilities. They have an eye for detail and are often excellent lawyers and diplomats.

The Hasta Nakshatra is believed to be one of the most fortunate and beneficiary stars in Vedic astrology. It provides the native with not only physical strength, but significant career elevation and advancements. It is also said to bring wealth and immense prosperity to the native's house.

The star Hasta is known to be a creative, intellectual and intuitive influence on the minds and spirits of its native. People born under this star are said to be masterful storytellers and great motivation speakers. They also possess strong organizational skills, both in managing diverse situations, yet staying harmoniously composed at the same time.

Further, it is believed that the Hasta Nakshatra gives its native success in any profession as long as dedication and focus are expressively portrayed. Since it is a central star, it marks success in the areas that it is connected to, such as in financial aspects, marriage, career or religious activities.

Essentially, the Hasta Nakshatra is one of the most beneficial and powerful stars in Vedic astrology and can bestow its native with immense success, prosperity and luck. Its influences are thus strongly pertinent to one's life and his/her ability to make choices that lead to a stronger future.

CHAPTER EIGHTEEN

CHITRA NAKSHATRA

(14 - Chithira)

Chitra nakshatra, or "Child of the Pleiades" has found a special place in Indian astrology and how it impacts the course of our lives. Located in the constellation of Virgo, Chitra Nakshatra is known for its hallowed symbols, a bright star composed of four small stars, a pearl, and a streak of light.

In Vedic Astrology, Chitra Nakshatra is a widely used parameter that has immense implications on studying a person's success and failures in life. When reading a person's birth chart, analyzing the position of Chitra Nakshatra gives a better understanding of the individual's inherent qualities, their personality traits and long-term effects of their minor and major decisions.

Generally speaking, this nakshatra is aligned with creativity, divinity and beauty. It is believed that those bom under the Chitra Nakshatra are blessed with natural aptitude for creativity. They should excel in performing arts, music, technology, good memory and healing arts.

People born under this nakshatra are often found to be much more confident and courageous than other nakshatras.

The traits of Chitra Nakshatra are equally evident in their lifestyle and thinking. These people are often seen to be exquisite, possess a magnetic personality and are better at controlling their emotions. Owing to their natural divine charm, they often tend to become the center of attraction.

In terms of health, people born under Chitra Nakshatra should take care of their sexual organs and reproductive system. Owing to their erratic nature, these people may take ill more often than other nakshatras. Mental health is a major concern and they should take more care in keeping their stress to a minimum.

The most important factor that makes Chitra Nakshatra valuable in astrology is its power to foretell the course of events and create unbelievable accuracy in predicting life events. Looking at the position of Chitra Nakshatra in a person's birth chart can actually give a broad idea about what one can expect in life in terms of both successes and failures.

In conclusion, it goes without saying that Chitra Nakshatra is a powerful astrological tool that has immense implications on how we live our lives. With its sprawling array of implications, it can be said that Chitra Nakshatra should be given its due importance and respect while studying one's birth chart.

CHAPTER NINETEEN

SWATI NAKSHATRA

(15 - Choti)

Swati Nakshatra is a significant and influential star of Vedic astrology. It is the 15th Nakshatra and the last Nakshatra of the animal kingdom. As part of the lunar calendar, Swati is associated with the liberation and spiritual oneness of the universe.

The literal meaning of Swati Nakshatra is "a star." It is represented as a plantain tree and is believed to yield results immediately after being worshipped. Swati also governs air, which reflects in its movements and takes on the shape of a wave.

Swati Nakshatra is closely associated with Buddhist and Hindu scriptures and is believed to have a tremendous spiritual power and influence. The thoughts and the activities followed by people under its influence is more inclined towards betterment and progress of the world.

Swati Nakshatra is the 15th Nakshatra in the Vedic lunar calendar. The deity associated with Swati Nakshatra is

Vayu, the god of wind. The symbols of Swati Nakshatra is a plantain tree. Swati is known to be associated with air and takes on the shape of a wave. Swati is associated with liberation and spiritual oneness, and governs mental and physical strength.

Swati Nakshatra is highly influential in both Hindu and Buddhist scriptures. It is believed to provide great spiritual power and influence to the individual, which can lead to the betterment and progress of the world.

The impact of Swati Nakshatra on individuals differs depending on the zodiac sign, placement of other planets and various other influences. Its influence leads to the strengthening of one's spiritual or mental side while also weakening the physical or emotional side.

By understanding and knowing the influence of Swati Nakshatra on an individual's life, an astrologer can be of great help in guiding the person and helping them lead a better life.

The role of Swati Nakshatra in astrology is to determine the characteristics and tendencies of someone's personality. It provides insight into the strengths and weaknesses of an individual.

Swati Nakshatra also helps in defining the feelings, emotions, ambitions and abilities of an individual. This helps in making decisions and planning for the future based on these attributes.

By understanding the effect of Swati Nakshatra, astrologers can assess the peronality traits, behavior patterns and life stages of an individual. They can also help in establishing peace and harmony in life.

In conclusion, Swati Nakshatra plays an important role in predicting one's future, knowing the strengths and weaknesses, and making the right choice in life. This can be immensely beneficial for charting out a path of success and happiness.

CHAPTER TWENTY

VISHAKA NAKSHATRA

(16 - Vaishakam)

Never heard of Vishaka Nakshatra? Don't worry, it is one of the oldest traditions of Hindu astrology and is a phenomenon that has been practiced for centuries. The meaning of Vishaka Nakshatra is "star of accomplishment" and is believed to be the star of good luck. It is said to carry within it, the power to bring prosperity and abundance to those who rely on its guidance.

Vishaka Nakshatra is one of the twenty-seven nakshatras, or lunar constellations, in Vedic astrology. It is primarily associated with the planet Jupiter and is located in the constellation of Libra. Vishaka Nakshatra represents the time period of 23° Libra to 6° Scorpio. It is also known as paush or purna, which means full or concerning the full moon. The ruling deity of the Vishaka Nakshatra is Indra, the Hindu god of thunder and rain.

Vishaka Nakshatra is an auspicious one, and is associated with accomplishments and good fortune. Individuals who are born under the Vishaka star are seen to be determined, goal-oriented and successful, as the star is said to open all doors of success. Due to this, Vishaka Nakshatra is considered highly auspicious according to Vedic Astrology. People of Vishaka Nakshatra are deemed energetic, ambitious, organized and hard-working, and because of such qualities, they tend to find success in every endeavor they undertake.

The ruling deity of Vishaka Nakshatra, Indra, is also associated with courage and risk-taking. This makes people born under Vishaka, fearless and willing to take chances. Such qualities are especially beneficial, especially in an ever-changing and competitive world.

Vishaka Nakshatra has been a key factor in Vedic Astrology for a long time and is an important tool for astrologers. Vishaka Nakshatra is used for different purposes such as prognostication, to ascertain the compatibility and future of two persons, to judge auspicious and inauspicious events, and to calculate the planetary transits.

Apart from this, Vishaka Nakshatra is also said to be beneficial in predicting important life events such as marriage, birth of a child, success and demise in business, and health issues. They help astrologers to accurately assess the past and the future, with the help of their predictions. Additionally, Vishaka Nakshatra is used to set karma and spiritual Astrology.

Vishaka Nakshatra, in a very real sense, has been an integral part of Vedic Astrology for centuries. It is said to potently bless its believers with luck, abundance and prosperity.

CHAPTER TWENTY-ONE

ANURADHA NAKSHATRA

(17 - Anizham)

Anuradha Nakshatra is an important star in the Indian Vedic astrological system. Also known as Anusham, Anuradha is the 17th Nakshatra in the traditional Hindu lunar zodiac. It covers a specific portion of the night sky, reflected by three stars in the constellation of Scorpio.

Anuradha Nakshatra is associated with a spear, symbolizing energy and metabolism. It is believed to reflect an individual's capacity for success and gaining material gains. People born under this nakshatra display a strong will for success and a great capacity for hard work. They have the aptitude to identify and tap into opportunities that present themselves. Anuradha Nakshatra's ruling deity is Mitra, the god of friendship and union, who symbolizes the qualities of harmony, generosity, and loyalty.

Anuradha rules over the kidneys and reproductive organs in the body and indicates vitality, dynamism and optimism when it impacts a natives horoscope. Anuradha also indicates career, finances, familial relationships, intelligence and strong sense of judgement. One born with Anuradha Nakshatra is creative, intuitive and detail-oriented, possessing great communication skills and ambition.

However, the effects of Anuradha Nakshatra can be both positive and negative depending on its placement in a native's birth chart. It can cause emotional distress and financial instability if it is conjunct malefic planets such as Rahu, Ketu, and Saturn or if it's in a malefic house or in negative aspect to another planet.

Anuradha Nakshatra's placement in one's horoscope is a very important factor for predicting their future. It is important for the astrologer to use both their analytical and intuitive knowledge to understand the effects of the star in a person's natal chart. Generally, it is said to be a beneficial Nakshatra, providing protection from disease, misfortune, and losses of all kinds. Those born under this star are thought to be successful in worldly affairs.

Anuradha Nakshatra truly reflects the power and potential of the individual's destiny. Those born under it are bound to defy odds and create success in all forms of life, be it in their personal and professional life. Thus, Anuradha Nakshatra remains an important star in the astrological system of India, imparting its profound influence and power on all aspects of a native's life.

CHAPTER TWENTY-TWO

JYESTHA NAKSHATRA

(18 - Thrikketta)

In astrology, Jyestha Nakshatra is one of the 27 Lunar Mansions or constellations and it is ruled by the planet Mercury. Generally considers as the 'eldest' of the Nakshatras, Jyestha is associated with power, authority, courage, and knowledge. It is represented by an eagle or umbrella and the deity of this Nakshatra is Indra, the chief of the gods.

Jyestha Nakshatra is known for its many admirable qualities such as ambition, will power and self-reliance as well as its more destructive elements of greed, jealousy, egoism, and violence. As a result of its various attributes, Jyestha nakshtra plays an important role in astrology and its influence can have a powerful effect on an individual's life.

First and foremost, Jyestha is considered to be the most favorable nakshatra for one's ascendant sign or "Lagna". People born under a favorable Jyestha lagna are usually quite successful and command respect from others. They are strong-willed and independent, able to handle difficult situations and make quick decisions. They have the ability to influence people and make sure they get what they want. Overall, those with a favorable Jyestha lagna tend to be quite fortunate in life.

The opposite is true for those born under an unfavorable Jyestha lagna. These individuals face challenges in their personal and professional life, such as delays in achievements, discouragements by others, and inability to complete tasks. Jyestha also influences one's financial situation and can bring bad luck if not handled well.

Additionally, Jyestha Nakshatra is known to have a beneficial effect on relationships. Those born under a favorable Jyestha lagna tend to have strong bonds with family and friends, and can make long-term relationships successful. People with an unfavorable Jyestha lagna, however, may struggle to maintain their relationships, or even to find someone to share their life with.

Finally, Jyestha Nakshatra has a great impact on one's destiny as well. It influences whether one will be successful in life or not and can determine certain events such as marriage, job change, etc. Those born under a favorable Jyestha lagna have better chances of success and can easily avoid obstacles that stand in their way. On the other hand, an unfavorable Jyestha lagna can block one's success and lead to unhappiness and lack of fulfillment.

In conclusion, Jyestha Nakshatra plays an important role in astrology. Its influence can have a major impact on one's life, influencing various elements such as relationships, finances, and destiny.

CHAPTER TWENTY-THREE

MOOLA NAKSHATRA

(19 - Moolam)

Moola Nakshatra has a significant role in the study of Indian astrology, often represented by its animal symbol: "the female rat or lamb." This constellation consists of four stars grouped together in the constellation of Scorpio, just south of the head of the Scorpion. Moola Nakshatra is one of the 27 nakshatras (constellations) that can be found in Jyotish, or Vedic astrology. It is believed to be a very powerful nakshatra, representing spirituality and is believed to bring great luck to those born under its influence.

Before exploring the facts, impact, and role of Moola Nakshatra in astrology, it's important to understand the basics of its origin and meaning. Moola means 'root', which gives a hint as to the purpose of this nakshatra. It's believed to be a powerful nakshatra in its ability to unlock the mysteries of the universe and remind us of the power of energy and the strong forces that exist within our lives that are not always visible.

On a more practical level, Moola Nakshatra is said to have a significant influence on matters related to marriage, business, and travel. It is believed to bring stability to these areas and ensure that decisions made are for the good of all. This constellation is also related to learning and education and is known to inspire difficult or tricky concepts.

When looking at the impact of Moola Nakshatra, we can see how it can influence things like career choices, health and wellness, and emotional stability. People born under Moola Nakshatra can be very determined individuals who have a strong sense of self-worth and a fearless approach to life. They have a better understanding of the intricacies of nature, the power of the Divine, and the importance of making decisions that are good for everyone.

The role of Moola Nakshatra in astrology should not be overlooked. Its impact on certain matters can be seen in many different ways. Firstly, it is important to note that it has a strong influence on individuals' karma and can encourage spiritual growth. Secondly, it can affect business and relationships, often bringing beneficial outcomes. Lastly, it can even lend its energy to matters related to travel and competition, often favouring its native over opponents.

To conclude, it is clear that Moola Nakshatra has an important role in astrology. It can be a source of insight, encouragement, and guidance. It can bring stability and luck to important matters related to marriage, business, and travel. It can also help introduce new ideas, spark creativity, and bring success in areas such as education and relationships.

CHAPTER TWENTY-FOUR

PURVASHADA NAKSHATRA

(20 - Pooradam)

Purvashada Nakshatra is an important factor in Vedic astrology, as it is one of the 27 fixed nakshatras within the zodiac. This nakshatra is preceded by Uttarashada and followed by Uttarashada and Shravana. The symbol of this nakshatra is a Golden Tower or two front legs of a bed, ruled by Vishnu and its symbol animal is a female mongoose.

Purvashada Nakshatra is a large and significant nakshatra in Vedic astrology. It's the twelfth sign of the zodiac and is located in the Sagittarius constellation. The moon passes through this nakshatra three times in one lunar month and covers 16-17 degrees of the zodiac. The ruling planet is Shukra (Venus). The deity associated with this nakshatra is Aryama, the ruler of the Pitris or ancestors.

Purvashada is an auspicious gemstone for many people and

is recognized for its blessings and powerful energy. The Nakshatra symbolizes blessings, good luck, wealth, accomplishment, growth and success. It allows one to access power and encourages harmony, family relationships, and spiritual progress. People born under the nakshatra of Purvashada have strong communication skills, good organizational abilities, and a strong desire for knowledge and growth. They are ambitious and have the ability to persist in whatever they aspire for. In addition, they are respected by others and have an attractive personality.

Role of Purvashada Nakshatra in Astrology: Purvashada Nakshatra has a major role to play in astrology. Its presence in a person's birth chart can show how they will achieve success in life. Those born under Purvashada, have a tendency to attract good opportunities and achieve their goals easily. It is also believed that this nakshatra provides positive energy and support in matters related to family and relationships. Purvashada is also known to bring good luck and helps the natives to live a prosperous life.

In conclusion, Purvashada is an important nakshatra in Vedic astrology. It is believed to bring luck, wealth and success, along with harmonious family relationships. The presence of Purvashada in a birth chart indicates a person's ability to achieve their goals and access power. Therefore, it is important to understand the role of Purvashada in astrology in order to find the right balance in life.

UTTARASHADA NAKSHATRA

(21 - Uthradam)

Uttarashada is an important star in Vedic astrology that plays an integral role in horoscope readings. It is the 21st nakshatra of the zodiac and is associated with the star Sadalmelik in the constellation Aquila. The symbol of Uttarashada is a fan or a hammer and it is ruled by the Sun.

Uttarashada is considered to be an auspicious star that provides its natives with a good start in life. It is associated with good fortune and is likely to bring wealth, power, and success for its natives. People born under this Nakshatra are believed to be highly knowledgeable, wise, and honest individuals. They are known for their confidence, ambition, and industrious nature, which often make them successful in their respective fields.

Uttarashada is a benevolent star and has a positive influence on the fortunes of its natives. It has the power to bestow tremendous wealth and an auspicious life. People born under this Nakshatra are believed to be lucky in gambling and other speculative activities. They are able to make quick gains through their intelligence and wisdom and often come out on top in difficult situations.

The role of Uttarashada in astrology is mainly determined by its placement in the horoscope. It influences the luck, fortunes, and destiny of the native. It can help the native achieve success and lead a prosperous life. It is also a powerful indicator of financial luck. When in auspicious positions, it can bring sudden gains, abundance, and wealth. On the other hand, when poorly placed, it can bring obstacles and losses.

Apart from its role in predicting the future, Uttarashada can also be used to provide remedies for difficult situations. It is believed that wearing jewels and gems associated with this star can help balance out problems caused by its negative placement in horoscopes and bring positive effects.

In conclusion, Uttarashada is an important star in Vedic astrology, with a powerful and positive influence on the lives of its natives. It has the ability to bring wealth and fortune and can help the native achieve success and lead a prosperous life. It can also be used to provide remedies for difficult situations.

CHAPTER TWENTY-SIX

SHARAVAN NAKSHATRA

(22 - Thiruvonam)

Shravan Nakshatra is an auspicious asterism in Vedic astrology. It is said to be the most important star sign in Hinduism, representing Lord Shiva, the destroyer and protector of the universe. Its Vedic name is Nakshatram, meaning 'star of good fortune', and it is associated with the principle of 'pride' and represents the highest power of the Supreme Self.

The Shravan Nakshatra is the seventh of the twenty-eight Nakshatras and stretches from the zodiacal sign of Cancer to the zodiacal sign of Uttara Ashadha, which spans 3°20' to 6°40'. Like all nakshatras, it is a star constellation and therefore, its location in the sky varies slightly. It is believed that when an individual is born in Shravan Nakshatra he or she will receive good luck and success and will be protected by Lord Shiva.

In astrological terms, the Shravan Nakshatra is associated

with the Pitri Paksha or Ancestral Worship which is focused on attending to the spiritual needs of one's ancestors. The sign is also associated with the Padma, or lotus, which is a symbol of beauty and prosperity. The color of Shravan Nakshatra is green and its ruling deity is Lord Vishnu.

Astrologers believe that this Nakshatra has a deep impact on the destiny of individuals who are born under it and that it determines the course of their life. It is believed that those born under Shravan Nakshatra will be blessed with wealth, intelligence, fame, respect, and good fortune.

In Vedic astrology, the Shravan Nakshatra is said to bring positive qualities such as enthusiasm, creativity, and determination. It is believed that individuals born under the Shravan Nakshatra will enjoy good health, be knowledgeable, have a good financial status, and be successful in their materialistic pursuits. It is said to aid individuals in discovering their own talents, understanding their spiritual path, and acquiring a better understanding of life.

The Shravan Nakshatra has long been revered by Hindus and its significance cannot be overstated. It represents harmony and peace and is believed to bring good luck and fortune to those born under it. Those who are born under the Shravan Nakshatra are sure to lead lives of joy and high achievement.

DHANISHTA NAKSHATRA

(23 - Avittam)

Dhanistha Nakshatra, also known as Shravan, is one of the 27 Nakshatras in Vedic astrology. It is the 23rd Nakshatra and is located in the constellation Aquila (Eagle). It is the ruling deity of this Nakshatra is the Lord of Wealth, Kubera, and its symbol is a drum.

Dhanistha Nakshatra is considered to be the most auspicious Nakshatra among the 27 Nakshatras in Vedic astrology. As the ruling deity is Kubera, the Lord of Wealth, it is believed to bring lot of financial prosperity, luck and abundance in one's life. This is the reason why it is considered so auspicious. The zodiac sign for Dhanistha Nakshatra is Sagittarius and its lord is Rahu. This Nakshatra is represented by the element of air and its ruling planet is Venus.

Dhanistha Nakshatra is believed to bring good luck, prosperity and abundance. People born in this Nakshatra are said to be obedient, patient and hardworking. They strive to achieve success with hard work and dedication. They also have a great sense of creativity and artistic talent. The people born in this nakshatra are very creative, energetic, and have the potential to become successful with their hard work and determination. They can be very influential and they have high potential to succeed in life.

Dhanistha Nakshatra is an important and auspicious nakshatra in Vedic astrology which has a powerful influence on a person's life. This Nakshatra gives immense strength to a person in terms of physical, mental, and spiritual power. People born in this Nakshatra are believed to have attractive personality, enhanced knowledge, and good luck associated with them. They can easily influence people and attract success in their life.

They are also known to find their way to their goals in life, and they can master their goals with correct guidance and knowledge. Dhanistha Nakshatra is associated with spiritual enlightenment, knowledge, and wisdom. People who are born in this nakshatra are said to be deeply spiritual, have deep faith in religion, and are creative.

In Vedic astrology, Dhanistha Nakshatra is associated with abundance and financial prosperity. It is also linked with luck, good fortune, and success. People born in this Nakshatra are said to be gifted, fortunate in terms of creative abilities, and proactive in their approach to life. This nakshatra is also associated with wealth, success, knowledge, and prosperity in all aspects of life.

CHAPTER TWENTY-EIGHT

SHATABISHA NAKSHATRA

(24 - Chathayam)

Shatabhisha Nakshatra is one of the 27 Nakshatras, or constellations, in the Hindu astrological system. It is governed by Rahu and is mainly associated with the water element, give it a mysterious and spiritual energy. Despite its deep and mysterious connotations, Shatabhisha Nakshatra is full of grounded stability and potential. From understanding its attributes to considering how it influences an individual's life, this Nakshatra is an important part of astrology.

First, it is important to understand the facts related to Shatabhisha Nakshatra. In Sanskrit, the word Shatabhisha is derived from two words: "Shata" meaning hundred and "bisha" meaning doctor. The Nakshatra consists of four stars located in Aquarius and its symbol is a riding animal or a circle. Its presiding deity is Varuna, the god of water, and its associated animal is a mongoose.

Now that we have established the facts of this Nakshatra, let's turn to its impact. Essentially, the qualities associated with Shatabhisha Nakshatra give an individual introspection, spiritual power, and truthful behavior. People born under this Nakshatra often take up a venture out of respect for their hard work, and eventually become successful. The fifth house in an individual's birth chart, which is governed by Shatabhisha Nakshatra, determines their intellect and wisdom. Thus, people belonging to this Nakshatra are usually highly intellectual, wise, and thoughtful.

Finally, we can consider how this Nakshatra plays a role in a person's life. Generally, Shatabhisha Nakshatra is associated with developing one's intuition, knowledge, and understanding of the world. People under this Nakshatra seek knowledge and strive to use it to benefit the world. Additionally, Shatabhisha Nakshatra is associated with divine wisdom and spiritual energy, which can help an individual to become a better person and to strive for greater realism and higher goals.

Overall, Shatabhisha Nakshatra is an important part of Hindu astrology. Its facts, impact, and role are integral to understanding an individual's life. The work ethic and spiritual energy associated with this Nakshatra make it a powerful tool for understanding the complexities of personal growth and potential.

PURVABHADRA NAKSHATRA

(25 - Pooruttathi)

Purvabhadra Nakshatra, also known as Poorvabhadrapad, is located in the constellation of Virgo. It belongs to the twilight group of Nakshatras, the first of 27 constellations in Hindu astrology. It is known for its power, energy, and influence in the astrological chart.

In Hindu astrology, Purvabhadra is the sign of energy and power. People born under this sign are said to be very intuitive, assertive, and confident. They are full of enthusiasm, ambition, and motivation. These qualities help them achieve their goals and move forward in life. They are also said to be determined, discipline, and organized. These traits make them very successful in their working environment.

In terms of fortune, the Purvabhadra Nakshatra is considered to be the most powerful sign. People born under this sign are said to be naturally lucky, and they enjoy success in every aspect of their lives. Due to its power and influence, Purvabhadra is also known as the Star of Wealth. Those born under this sign are typically happy and prosperous. It is also said to be a sign of strength and power.

When it comes to the relationship between planets, Purvabhadra Nakshatra has an important role to play. It is said to be a factor in the compatibilities of planets when in the same house. In its basic form, planets in the same house are more likely to produce positive results, while those in different houses are more likely to produce discordant results.

The Purvabhadra Nakshatra has an impact on various aspects of a person's life such as education, career, family, and relationships. It helps determine how strong will a person be. It is believed that people who possess this Nakshatra will have a strong will and determination, which will ultimately help them in the pursuit of their goals.

In conclusion, the Purvabhadra Nakshatra is a powerful sign in Hindu astrology. It is said to have a great impact on a person's life in terms of wealth, strength, and power. It also plays a crucial role in determining the compatibility of planets and their effect on a person's life. All these reasons make Purvabhadra Nakshatra an important part of astrology.

CHAPTER THIRTY

UTTARABHADRA NAKSHATRA

(26 - Uthruttathi)

Uttarabhadra is an important concept in the study of astrology. It is a star located near the north pole of the heavens that is astrologically imbued with astronomical importance. Widely studied and discussed since ancient times, the star and its constellation represent the heavens and the divine nature of existence in the celestial realm.

The root of the term 'Uttarabhadra' is believed to stem from the Sanskrit language, with reference to the north pole of the heavens. Specifically, the term 'Uttara' means 'north', while 'bhadra' is defined as 'prosperous'. Therefore, the star and its zodiac signify wealth, abundance, and celestial guidance and direction in traditional astrology.

Astronomical facts relating to the star and its zodiac have been established. Uttarbhadra is located at the twenty-fourth degree of the Aquarius zodiac. It is, on average, around 380 times brighter than Sirius, the brightest star in the night sky. Furthermore, the star and its zodiac are thought to be associated with the animals elephant and peacock, respectively.

The study of Uttarabhadra and its position within the zodiac is important in the field of astrology. As with other stars and their associated zodiacs, the location of Uttarabhadra can impact significantly on human life. For instance, the placement of the star is believed to determine the luck and fortune associated with major life events and decisions, as well as a signification of fortune and good luck.

In reference to astrological predictions and application, Uttarabhadra and its associated eleventh house of the Aquarius zodiac are believed to impact on events such as the success of a business venture, the prospects for financial prosperity, and long-term partnerships and relationships.

In conclusion, Uttarabhadra and its associated zodiac are an important component of astrology. A subject that has been studied and discussed since ancient times, the star has many associated astronomical and astrological facts, which are believed to have an impact on events and decisions in life. It is thus an important concept in the field of astrology.

REVATI NAKSHATRA

(27 - Revathi)

Revati nakshatra is one of the most important nakshatras in Vedic astrology. It is the 27th nakshatra of the zodiac and it belongs to the Pisces sign in Vedic astrology. In Indian astrology, Revati nakshatra is associated with Masculine energy and is ruled by the planet Mercury and the god Pushan. It is believed that the influence of Revati nakshatra can be seen in all aspects of one's life.

Revati nakshatra is believed to bring many beneficial effects in one's life. it is believed to bring clarity in one's thought process, helping one to make more accurate decisions. Its presence also provides stability to an individual, helping them to stay focused on the task at hand and be successful in their endeavors.

In Vedic astrology, Revati nakshatra possess the qualities of the rashi or sign of the same name. Its qualities include intelligence, intuition, creativity, and the ability to think outside the box. It is believed that persons born with this nakshatra are often blessed with considerable wealth and abundant resources. They possess an inner strength that helps them to remain stable in the face of adversity and any difficult situation.

The role of Revati nakshatra in astrology is of utmost importance. It is believed that the nakshatra influences an individual's nature, their thoughts, behavior and luck in life. People born with Revati nakshatra often have a peaceful and pleasant nature and are fair in their dealings. They are often able to achieve any task they set their mind too and possess the inner strength to face any adversity.

In terms of career, Revati nakshatra individuals are often successful in life as well. They are often highly ambitious, creative and are adept at devising strategies that help them to make the most of their abilities. They also tend to excel in various fields such as writing, communications, and marketing.

In conclusion, Revati nakshatra has a great impact on an individual's life and character. It is associated with many beneficial effects and its qualities help individuals to achieve greater success in their respective fields. It helps them to think more clearly and make better decisions. The people born with Revati nakshatra often make good inroads in terms of their career, wealth and overall success.

Other Books Of The Author

1. The Moments When I Met God
2. Kashiyile Theertha Pathangal
3. GURU GYAN VANI
4. Abhiprerak Gita
5. ASSI SE JAIN GHAT TAK
6. Hopelessness of Arjuna
7. The Soul and It's True Nature
8. Sense of Action (Karma)
9. Action through Wisdom
10. Action through Wisdom
11. THEORY AND PRACTICAL OF EVERY ACTION
12. LOGICAL UNDERSTANDING OF THE SUPREME
13. THE IMPERISHABLE SUPREME
14. Yatra Nishadraj se Hanuman Ghat Tak
15. Yatra Karnatak Ghat se Raja Ghat Tak
16. Yatra Pandey Ghat se Prayagraj Ghat Tak
17. Yatra Ranjendra Prasad Ghat se Dattatreya Ghat Tak
18. YaatraSindhiya Ghat se Gwaliar Ghat Tak
19. Yatra Mangala Gauri Ghat se Hanuman Gadhi Ghat Tak
20. Yatra Gaay Ghat Se Nishad Ghat Tak
21. MAA GANGA, GHATEN EVM UTSAV
22. Ganga Arti Dev Deepavali evam Any Utsav
23. Potentials of Digitalized India
24. VEDIC CONSCIOUSNESS
25. A Brief Introduction to Vedic Science
26. Kashi ke Barah Jyotirling
27. IMPACT OF MOTIVATION
28. Let's have a Milky Way Journey
29. Color Therapy in a Nutshell

30. Rigveda in a Nutshell
31. Yajurveda in a Nutshell
32. Samveda in a Nutshell
33. Atharva Veda in a Nutshell
34. Ayushman Bhava - on Ayurveda
35. Srimad Bhagavad Gita and Upanishad Connection
36. Facts and Impact of Nakshatras

Contact

DR. JAGADEESH PILLAI

PhD in Vedic Science

Four Times Guinness World Record Holder

Winner of Mahatma Gandhi Vishwa Shanti Puraskar and Global Peace Ambassador

Gemology, Astro & Vastu Consultant - Spiritual Counselor

Consultant for designing World Record Ideas

9839093003

myrichindia@gmail.com

drjagadeeshpillai@facebook

drjagadeeshpillai@instagram

jagadeeshpillai@youtube

www. JAGADEESHPILLAI.com